Into the Wildfire:
Mourning Departures

By Noor Shirazie

Into the Wildfire: Mourning Departures

By Noor Shirazie

Copyright © 2016 Noor Shirazie
All rights reserved. No part of this book may be reproduced or transmitted in any form or by any means, electronic or mechanical, including photocopying, recording or by any information storage and retrieval system, without the prior and express written permission of the author.

First published: 2016

To my mother, the inspiration behind the pen.

To the people, the memories, the stories behind the poetry.

To those that struggle to find their voice.

To those that cannot put their pain, their anger, their hope,

their faith into words—

this is for you.

Mourning Departures

If only I had known
how quickly the days would elapse,
how small the window of time would be
in which I could have told you
how much you truly mean to me.

Know it now—
I love you,
    I love you,
        I love you.

The hour is late,
you have one foot out the door,
but I do love you.

Scatter my promises
like ashes toward the watchful sun.
Let them decorate the sky so that
the clouds dissolve every part of us.

Look upward and remember
that you and I were truly something.

Your hands tremble uncontrollably,
and you throw up more often.
You do not have an appetite anymore
but need to eat to keep your diminishing strength intact.

You are relentlessly fading away,
regardless of what the doctors say.
I try to keep your spirit up,
but we both know that very soon,
there will not be a spirit to preserve.

Forgive me for the moments
I undermined so carelessly.
I thought we would have more time.
I cannot bear to watch you
        so weak,
   so frail,
but do not think for a second
that I will leave your side.

You are where my joy lies,
and if you run out of hope
on which to lean,

        lean on me.

His voice still hangs in the air
like an eerie tune—
slightly off-key,
but it is the kind of sound
you memorize and never forget.

His faded fingerprints still clutter
the windows of my soul,
and I have given absolutely everything
to try and wipe them away.
Maybe I am destined
to watch him taint everything I see.
Maybe anything I ever love is bound
to have his name engraved into it.

I sense him in the lost crevices of my heart,
abandoned alleyways which have not
known the rhythm of footsteps in centuries.
I see him too clearly to ever let him
become a distant memory.
I feel him too vividly to ever let my hand
brush the hand of another.

There is a world inside of him
that I was not patient enough to discover.

I will keep revisiting him
long after I know I should stop,
the same way the moon greets the sun
during every lunar eclipse.

I will never fall
into another human being
the way I did for him.

Goosebumps litter my skin, spelling out
it has always been him
as I recall what I will never
bring myself to leave behind.

He is the end of me.

Denial compels me to run after a train
well on its way to another station.
Burning a bridge is not always easy
when you trust someone to build it with you
from the strongest steel.

No matter how diligently
I try to forget you, my hands
keep opening this book to your pages.

Not for lack of trying,
I cannot smooth over the ripples
that this disaster of a heartbreak has caused.
The rough edges have become the only surface
my fingertips have ever known.

To be blank again would mean
repeating every mistake that ever
taught me how to survive.

You are the chapter I can never escape.

You gave yourself away
within your table of contents,
leaving him with no interest
in the remainder of the book.

Do not weep over losing him,
but for the parts of yourself
that are forever lost with him.
Indulge your imagination
by pretending you meant something to him,
if only for a passing moment.

The tennis ball-sized lump in your throat
is the reason you have remained speechless
from the time he left till the time
you stopped seeing him in every place
that still means something to you.

He knows all too well
that you still search for the missing piece
that he keeps with him.

You are too afraid to retrieve
the last piece of the puzzle,
so you wander in search of it
in those whom you know do not possess it,
wasting your time and fortifying the barrier
that you have not been able to dissolve.

Overdone,
    overused—
every thought in your mind has been laid to rest,
    every sentiment written to death.
Your past is as exhausted as you have become.

Know that, after all that you have endured,
nobody is forcing you to be strong
when you have every right to crumble.

I could talk endlessly about certain people.
I keep them safe in the core of my heart,
proud to share memories of them
with everyone I encounter.

And then there is you.

When anyone brings up
the shadow of your name,
I am parched like earth which has been
without water for far too long.

I become quiet,
filled with a blur of remorse
that should have been voiced but never was.
I try not to flinch as I wait
for the pain in my hollow chest to subside,
but it forever remains,
stirring whenever my thoughts
accidentally trip over you.

"I meant no harm," you hurriedly told me
as I crumpled to the floor,
the weight of everything you said
crushing my bones.

If this is the damage you cause
when you mean no harm,
how many earthquakes await
in the folds of your unadulterated rage?

It was us against the world,
until you brought mine
to a sudden halt.
If you are to fracture me,
have enough decency
to look me in the eye while doing so.

Watch my slow,
    inevitable
        collapse.

Some stars glow brighter than others,
       more brilliant,
            more insistent.
The light you absorb fills you to the brim,
and you could burst with life
at any given moment.

But what happens when
you encounter the brightest one of all?

What happens when it passes you by,
and you can feel warmth draining
from skin that tries desperately
to cling to the last traces of heat?

You were my star.

I could spend an eternity
scouring the galaxies,
but I will never come across anyone
who shone like you.

Time is the thief that harbors no regrets.
It leaves those burdens with us.
I will never know what haunts me more—
the things I valued
or the moments lost
in an attempt to acquire them.

Regret is a silent arrow.

My mind shoots its crossbow
in the quietest hour of night.
If you listen intently,
you can hear the tail whistle
before it greets its target.

I want to disintegrate
and fall back into easier times,
like a bad habit
I once had control over.

I reach hungrily for the past
as it taunts my senses,
but it will never come alive in my grasp.

If anything, it may just die out faster.

Being near you now
would be far too dangerous for us both.

Let us pretend things ended peacefully,
even when the storm inside me
has pushed away anything that
remotely resembles peace.
The gashes are still too fresh to cover
with lies and false reassurances.

This is not okay.
What you did was not okay.
It was not departure,
    it was reckless abandonment.

I am still finding my way to forgiveness,
but for now, all I know is that
I face a very real risk of breaking completely
at the thought of being
in your excruciating presence.

I hope you question every reason for leaving,
no matter how carefully constructed they may be.

I hope I plant enough doubts in your mind
to counter the many sleepless nights
you cruelly left me with.

Tormented by remembering,
    tortured by forgetting—
she is the master of reincarnation,
dying each time her thoughts dwell upon him.

It is incredible how
the mouth that whispers,
"I can't live without you"
between bedsheets
is the same mouth to end it all,
telling her she was never enough.

Be kind enough to glue
the petals you ripped from her body
back onto her bare skin.

Do not leave her naked
and susceptible to your inhumanity,
just because she was brave enough
to undress in front of you.

Only someone like you could utter a goodbye
and make it feel like the sky were falling.

As you exit the corridor
with fingernails scratching against
the barren sides of both walls,
remember to lock the door on your way out.
This heart has run out of space
to store further wreckage.

Erase me.
   Delete us.

Look at your face with utter confusion
and wonder where all those kisses originated.
Look at your hands and wonder
why they appear so empty without mine in them.
Look at your loneliness and wonder
why the void within it is yet to be filled.

Even without me to help you
remember what you are about to lose,
you know there is something missing.

Even though I outgrew you
like a shrunken sweater,
I still like to open up the closet
in the neglected corner of my room
and reminisce what fit me perfectly
once upon a time.

My nails dig hard and fast
into the final traces of you
before the fragments are whisked away
into the hands of someone new.

Exhale slower, my darling.

I fear you will be gone
as quickly as it takes
for breath to leave the body.

"Take care of him,"
I shall whisper to her,
praying she keeps you safe
in her locket of a heart.

It is the most basic of human yearnings,
to be honored long after
we deserve to be forgotten.

Maybe if our fingers did not
interlock as perfectly as they used to,
if our sentences were not
completed by each other,

I would be able to forget you.

But all those things happened.
They were real,
      you were real.

You have built yourself
a fortress in my memory,
and I do not intend
to evict you anytime soon.

Tell me we were more
than words on a page.
Remind me that we were as sweet
as the taste of each poem on my tongue.

In a crowd of hundreds,
I still find myself
searching for familiarity
with which I never grew up,
hands that should have held my own
as I learned how to walk,
warmth that should have
read me bedtime stories
and sung me sweet lullabies.

Although I cannot forgive the merciless years
for robbing me of a father
that should have protected my innocence,
I cannot stop myself from missing
what was never there,
for craving comfort of which
every child should know.

The sound of letting something slip from my grasp
is the most frustrating,
    gut-wrenching sound imaginable,
not only because I held onto something
once upon a time, but because
it had an urge to escape from me.

He writes, *"I am leaving"*,
each letter obnoxiously capitalized.
I write, *"but I need you to stay"*
in cursive, hoping the words
flow smoothly enough
for him to change his mind.

Know that I shall never
be reignited by another again.
My spark shall die with you.

If you must go, remember
to pack all your unkept promises
into that hasty suitcase.
Do not leave any space for me to miss you.

Even if I were to throw
any of your belongings
into the hungry flames,
I know you shall never leave me in peace.

If you stay, I will fade slowly.
If you go, it will take but an instant
before I disappear completely,
lost to anyone and anything that ever
had the misfortune of knowing
a broken individual.

Shame on me for letting you
define all that I was,
          all that I am.

My brain is ever so talented
at channeling mixed signals—
to stay,
   not to stay,
      to have one foot out the door
         and another in a roomful of chaos.

Every intertwining moment with you
slowly pushes me toward the terrifying realization.
It hits me like a freight train and slowly sinks in—

I do not know how to forget you.
It cannot be learned, nor willed.
You are with me, for better or worse.

I shudder to speak of you,
but sadly, that does not mean
I dream of you any less.

Familiar waters run deep.

I replay the memories like an old cassette,
one that can never be thrown away
no matter how damaged the tape becomes.
The river may have run dry,
but the damp soil has not forgotten
how freely the current once flowed.

He and I are too familiar
to call ourselves strangers.
That would mean erasing
a lifetime of shared hope,
    combined grief,
overlapping laughter.

He is the end to my beginning.

I can still recall
the rhythm of his breathing
as his chest rose and fell.
It is a beat I cannot bring myself to forget.

Do not force me to forget.

My playlists are cluttered
with sad songs and fractured memories,
yet I unconvincingly claim I am trying to move on.

Love places its hands over my eyes—
clouding my judgement,
    causing hallucinations,
        making me say things that are so unlike me.

It is not a feeling.
It is not a drug.
It is the devil on my shoulder,
egging me on to commit new crimes,
urging me to create new reasons to suffer silently.

Inhaling, letting you corrupt every pore—
your ashtray kisses will forever
leave burns on my weathered skin.
Your toxicity destroys me,
but not breathing you in
will be what finally kills me.

My fingertips are stained,
permanently changed after knowing your skin.

This cliff is far too steep.
I do not possess the bravery to fall with you.
I am sorry for being so damn terrified of heights.

Some call it moving forward,
    others call it being forced to forget.
Either way, our spirit feels as heavy as our feet
when we must leave someone we love a little too soon,
    when they must leave us.

I burn thoughts of you to the ground
but protect the ashes.
Even in their most unwanted form,
the blackened recollections
will always be of value to me.

Who is to say
we will not meet again
in the middle of our demise?

All these people,
these broken relationships,
smother me in my sleep.

Too close, one gets hurt.
Too far, one is not hurt enough.
I cannot seem to breathe in clean air.

"What changed you?"
The lump in my throat forms faster
than my ability to provide an answer.

I leave bits of home in those that never return.
Goodbyes—the gunshot amidst silence,
the sting before returning to a reality once deserted.

There is a dusty museum
within my weathered soul,
a collection of relics that take up space
better spent on here and now.

My pen transports me to places I would rather leave behind.
Confused, I ask, *"Why did you bring me back here?"*
Knowingly, the pen answers with a loaded question—
"Why do you still write of him?"

The calendar on my wall is filled with red pen marks,

scarlet indicators of days on which
I force myself to reluctantly remember it all.

September 15th, the day life stopped altogether.
December 21st, beginning to recollect
pieces of who I was before you.

February 3rd, between relapse and trauma.

May 8th, learning to breathe without your oxygen.
August 2nd, a dash of lingering hope in the air.
November 15th, soaring and
barely able to notice you in hindsight.

I dream of the day I will no longer scribble
any red reminders to forget you,
    to move on,
        to live.

"How did you have the strength to hold on?"
"How did you have the audacity to let go?"

Your words strike me like landmines.

I am too afraid to take a step,
fearful that there will not be anything left of me
by the time this conversation is over.
There is a graveyard for every unspoken word.
Each syllable is left to face an inevitable death,
far from the person for whom it was meant.

You and I are a tale from ancient times,
but I am too afraid to wipe off the memories
and flip through our pages.

Words will only amplify
an injury too deep for poetry.

Like a shooting star,
your disappearance came about
as quickly as your sudden arrival,
but that did not make you
any less of a wonder.

The sun has set on you and I,
but I will never forget
how striking the evening looked
before our twilight.

These loose ends fall around me in disarray.
The moment I try to tie them up,
more knots begin to slowly unravel.
Is it even worth chasing the past
when these mistakes excel
at hunting me down?

Teach me how to read you
as the closed book you are.

Curse our bitter ending.
    I know I do.

I was nothing but a nomad to you.

Destined to leave,
    inclined to stay.
I would have gladly rewritten
my entire journey for you,
but you already viewed me as a traveler.

"Wait for me," you murmured,
with no intention of ever returning.
I was your right now
after you became my infinity.
Home is a comfort that
walked away when you did.

Time makes no effort to heal
this deep gash of a wound,
so I take matters into my own hands—

stitching it up on my own,
    doing more harm than good.

If I tear out specific pages from my past,
the entire spine may collapse.
You are the sentence I left incomplete,
    the page I left unwritten—
        forever fragmented and unfinished.

Tell me that I left a footprint in your life,
    that there is some part of me
    that can never truly disappear,
        that I changed you for the better.

Tell me that I made
a shred of difference to you,
    that she has not washed away everything
    I am scared you may have forgotten.

Do not allow us to deteriorate
from reminiscence to regret.

I glance down at the photograph of you and I,
    rip it down the middle,
and acknowledge that
I will never separate you from my thoughts,
no matter how far apart
I keep the two halves of that picture.

How ironic—
    out of all the people to feel like home,
              you did.
      Out of all the people to uproot my home,
            you did.

Your name only adds salt
to these gaping wounds.
I size up everyone I meet,
but they only seem to shrink
as they are measured against you.

Maybe I expect too much of them.

Maybe you have spoiled me to the point
that nobody else will ever be as memorable.

Because you vanished as quickly as you appeared,
I will always doubt your ability to stay.
I want so badly for you
to become native to a country
that will always seem foreign to you.

I am sorry we cannot
understand each other's hearts
as well as we had hoped.

It is one thing to recite poetry,
but not everyone can fill each syllable
with as much meaning as you did.
It is a rare gift,
one that will fade with
my many memories of you.

When my enthusiasm for love
dies out completely,
I want them to engrave your name
into the headstone.

"There's nothing left to say,"
I hurriedly exclaim
before the waterfall of regrets and apologies
spill from a mouth that wants to do nothing
but kiss the disaster better.

Each heartbeat pulsates with a thousand words
I did not say to you when the time was right.
What could have been will kill me
in the peak of twilight,
when there is nothing to distract me
from the way things could have worked out.

Is it too aggressive of me to say
I want to rip the past into shreds?
I cannot change how I feel,
and you cannot change
how catastrophically this ended.

I do not want to remember anything—
not you,
    not how my heart heals differently now.

I want you to stop existing in the past
as easily as you stopped existing in my future.

They say all cravings pass with time,
but to give you up is to demand the impossible.
You may be miles away,
but I still listen for your pulse wherever I go.

I want to be more than just a memory,
but one cannot be forced
to remember others a certain way
if they view the past in different colors.

While there are tornadoes that I choose to store
in the neglected corners of my mind,
it does not mean they did not happen.
    It does not mean you did not happen.

To the naked eye,
your silhouette begins fading to black.
To my heart, you never left.

Your absence fuels
my desperate desire to keep you alive.

I romanticized you to the point that
the knives you pressed into my skin
began to look like Cupid's arrows.

I let you change me in
the worst and most permanent of ways.
I trusted you with responsibilities that
should not have been delegated to anyone else.

Part of it was fear,
    part of it was hope.
I wanted you to be the answer to everything
when I was too anxious to face my own questions.

The rose speaks not of its troubles
on the way to blooming,
but you can still notice the trauma
upon its distressed petals.

You taught me how to sing
but left before I could envelop you in music.

Do not whisper me lullabies
and then abruptly disappear.
I prefer to awaken in the middle of the night
to a warm body than an absence
whose chill still lingers in the sleeping air.

For someone that injected so much
familiarity and comfort into my life,
it truly feels as if you have
ripped apart my very home.

I feel nauseous just thinking about
the rubble that is yet to be cleared.

You reside in crevices that you no longer deserve,
corners of my being that cannot endure
another letdown by your vicious hands.

Your laugh never fully recovered
from all the devastation,
and it takes everything inside of you
to produce a weak smile in the face of torment.

Your expression states that you have forgotten him,
but your heart is not as unforgiving.

"How did you bring yourself to heal?"
I asked, after noticing the lived days upon your face.
The uneasy silence told me
that the torment has not yet subsided.
The skeletons in your closet rattle most loudly
when you believe you have shut them out.

You were never a good liar.
It shows when you claim to have forgotten him.

*"Why is it that you are so disappointed
by each person that comes your way?"*
*"Because they are walking reminders
that they will never match up to you."*

And they never do.

Some of them have eyes that resemble yours.
Maybe that is why I am compelled to lower my gaze.
Some of them are as carefree as you are,
but it does not matter.

I cannot blossom twice
after flourishing around you.

Your name is a Pandora's box,
demanding to be opened.
I shudder to think of what I may find.

I have thought about it all, long and hard.
The blame weighs down on me like a ton of bricks,
and I start to believe our divide is all my fault.
"I did this, I did this,"
sobbing to myself over and over again.

The truth ceases to matter.

As he inched further away from her,
she tightened her grip on his hand,
unwilling to let go.

*"If he wants his hand back,
he'll have to stay,"* she thought.

He looked up at her apologetically,
let his hand turn limp in hers,
and slowly slid it from her grip.
She let him leave,
still unable to comprehend
what just took place.

But then it hit her.

You cannot hold on to a person
when they do not wish to be held.

It is as simple and as terrifying as that.

In psychology, object permanence
describes how something continues to exist
even when it cannot be
seen, heard, touched, or smelled.

Little does everyone know
that you cease to exist to me,
yet I still sense you everywhere.
I hear echoes of you in the rain,
        in the air,
in the very sunlight that seeps
into my yearning flesh.

Every storm forces me to recall
what I force myself to leave behind.

You are the furniture
I keep knocking my shin against
when I assume the coast is clear.

My limbs cannot endure another bruise.

I followed you down an abyss,
but only one of us returned.
I will not forgive the way you left me
with a smirk on your cunning face.

We view places as transitory,
yet they hold a place in us.
Maybe I will not hurt as deeply
if I view you the same way—
impermanent,
    fleeting,
        casually passing through.

You were never meant to stay, were you?

Upon your departure,
I have learned to breathe again,
the way I did before ever knowing you—
but oh, how my bones still ache.

Too often, goodbyes are ripped out of us
before they can be heard.

An empty apology does not bring closure.

I am falling into despair,
unable to determine whether to hold on
or let your phantom slip further away.
It taints everyone I know.
Everyone begins to resemble you,
and yet, they will only plant weeds
where you once grew a bed of roses.

Who knew you and I were so horribly brittle?

I am broken glass.
I am the questions you leave unanswered
in the corner of the room.
I am a fragment of what I worked so hard for.

Damn you for stealing away
so much of who I once was.

The sound of that door closing
haunts me more
than the voice I shall never hear again.

How do the bruises manage to hurt
years after they were inflicted?
I continuously stumble
into new layers of agony,
unsure of whether I will ever resurface.

I was never a skilled player
when it came to your wicked games.
Maybe you can help me perfect
the art of breaking someone slowly.

I hope you and your conscience
sit in the middle of the night
and discuss past crimes for hours on end.

The past is much like airports that never sleep—
clusters of *hellos* and *goodbyes*,
the agony of parting,
  the joy of being reunited.

They return as quickly as they leave,
often with static noise
and explanations that never
do the abandonment justice.

This time, I refuse to go quietly.

If we are to end this,
you will allow me
to mourn from the rooftop,
    crumble with enough fury to shake the earth,
        compose myself with enough dignity to impress us both.

We shall move on,
but not before I respect us enough
to give this the farewell it deserves.

Printed in Poland
by Amazon Fulfillment
Poland Sp. z o.o., Wrocław